BEHIND THE SCE
BIOGRAPHIES

WHAT YOU NEVER KNEW ABOUT

>>> —————— <<<

STEPHEN

CURRY

by Dr. Nafeesah Allen

CAPSTONE PRESS
a capstone imprint

This is an unauthorized biography.

Spark is published by Capstone Press, an imprint of Capstone
1710 Roe Crest Drive, North Mankato, Minnesota 56003
capstonepub.com

Library of Congress Cataloging-in-Publication Data
Names: Allen, Nafeesah, author.
Title: What you never knew about Stephen Curry / by Dr. Nafeesah Allen.
Description: North Mankato, Minnesota : Capstone Press, [2024] | Series: Behind the scenes biographies | Includes bibliographical references and index. | Audience: Ages 9 to 11 | Audience: Grades 4-6 | Summary: "Stephen Curry has wowed fans with his incredible basketball skills, including three NBA championships. But what is his life like off the court? High-interest details and bold photos of his fascinating life will enthrall reluctant and struggling readers, while carefully levelled text will leave them feeling confident"— Provided by publisher.
Identifiers: LCCN 2022058760 (print) | LCCN 2022058761 (ebook) | ISBN 9781669049470 (hardcover) | ISBN 9781669049241 (paperback) | ISBN 9781669049258 (pdf) | ISBN 9781669049272 (kindle edition) | ISBN 9781669049289 (epub)
Subjects: LCSH: Curry, Stephen, 1988- —Juvenile literature. | Basketball players—United States—Biography—Juvenile literature. | Guards (Basketball)—United States—Biography—Juvenile literature. | Golden State Warriors (Basketball team)—History—Juvenile literature.
Classification: LCC GV884.C88 A45 2024 (print) | LCC GV884.C88 (ebook) | DDC 796.323092 [B]—dc23/eng/20221214
LC record available at https://lccn.loc.gov/2022058760
LC ebook record available at https://lccn.loc.gov/2022058761

Editorial Credits
Editor: Mandy Robbins; Designer: Heidi Thompson; Media Researcher: Jo Miller; Production Specialist: Tori Abraham

Image Credits
Alamy: ZUMA Press, Inc., 4; Associated Press: Charles Krupa, 25; Getty Images: Elsa, Cover, Jed Jacobsohn, 17, Jonathan Ferrey, 22, Matt Winkelmeyer, 18, Noah Graham, 9, 28-29 (both), Ronald Martinez, 21, STEPHANIE AGLIETTI, 27; San Francisco Chronicle via AP: Lance Iversen, 6, Michael Macor, 12; Shutterstock: Epov Dmitry, 14, hanzl, 7 (bottom), Igor Dutina, 13, Iris Joschko, 26, Lightspring, 7 (top), PchelaMajka, 19, Tinseltown, 11, Yeti studio, 14-15

All internet sites appearing in back matter were available and accurate when this book was sent to press.

Printed and bound in China. PO5379

TABLE OF CONTENTS

A Champ with Many Names 4

All in the Family 6

Pop Quiz! 10

The Real Chef Curry 12

Steph's Second Sport 16

Curry's MVPs 18

Giving Back 24

    Glossary 30

    Read More 31

    Internet Sites 31

    Index 32

    About the Author 32

Words in **bold** are in the glossary.

A CHAMP WITH MANY
NAMES

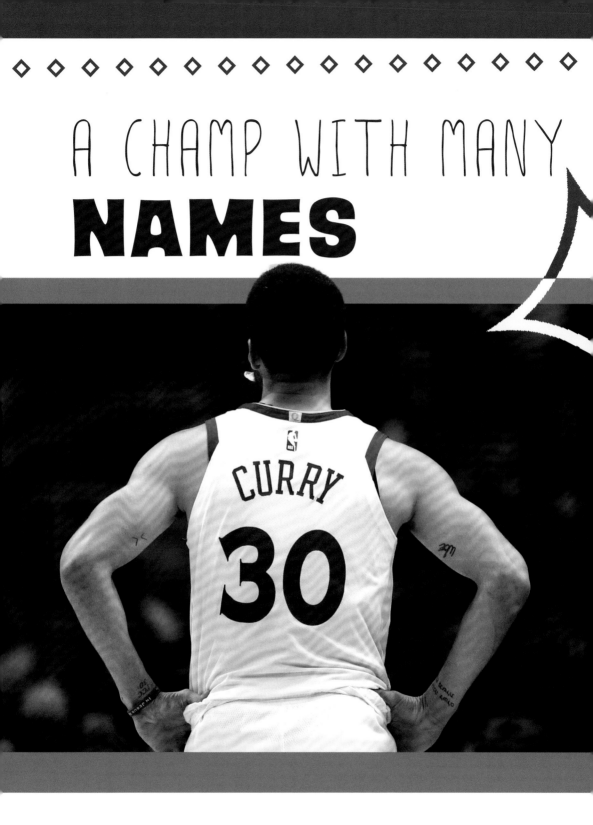

Three-time NBA champion Stephen Curry is often called Steph Curry. Do you know his other nicknames? Some call him the Baby-Faced **Assassin**. The rapper Drake refers to him as Chef Curry. Friends and family call him Wardell or Dell. Why? Wardell Jr. is his first name. Stephen is his middle name.

What else might surprise you about Steph Curry? Find out!

ALL IN THE
FAMILY

Dell, Steph, and Sonya Curry

Steph's talent comes naturally! He got his hoop skills from his dad, Dell Curry. He played pro basketball too. Steph got his *hops* from his mom, Sonya. She was a volleyball player for Virginia Tech college.

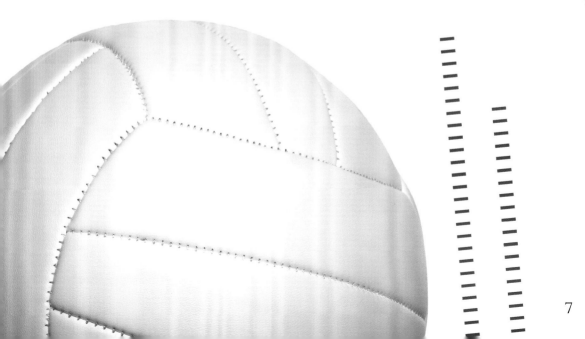

The rest of the family has sports skills too. Steph's sister, Sydel, played volleyball at Elon University in North Carolina. Steph's brother, Seth, won't be left out! He plays for the Brooklyn Nets.

FACT

Steph's sister, Sydel, is married to Phoenix Suns star Damion Lee.

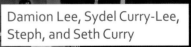
Damion Lee, Sydel Curry-Lee, Steph, and Seth Curry

POP QUIZ!

Time for a pop quiz about Steph Curry!

1. **When and where was Steph Curry born?**

2. **What other NBA legend was born in the same hospital?**

3. **How old was Steph when he met his wife, Ayesha?**

4. **What does he write on his sneakers?**

5. **What do fans call Steph Curry and Klay Thompson?**

1. March 14, 1988 in Akron, Ohio 2. LeBron James 3. 15 years old
4. a Christian quote: *I can do all things.* 5. The Splash Brothers

THE REAL
CHEF CURRY

Ayesha Curry

"Chef Curry" cooks up great plays on the basketball court. But his wife, Ayesha, is the real cook. Steph loves her chicken parmesan. And she loves that he loves it.

What about snacks? Steph has a weakness for popcorn. He's even ranked the popcorn sold at different stadiums.

When it comes to sweet treats, Steph loves Sour Patch Kids. The candies remind him of his childhood!

STEPH'S
SECOND SPORT

Can you guess what sport Steph Curry would play if he weren't playing basketball? Golf! And Steph has the skills to back it up. He's even golfed with President Obama.

Steph is also a big fan of his friend, golfer Rory McIlroy! They played together in **charity** tournaments.

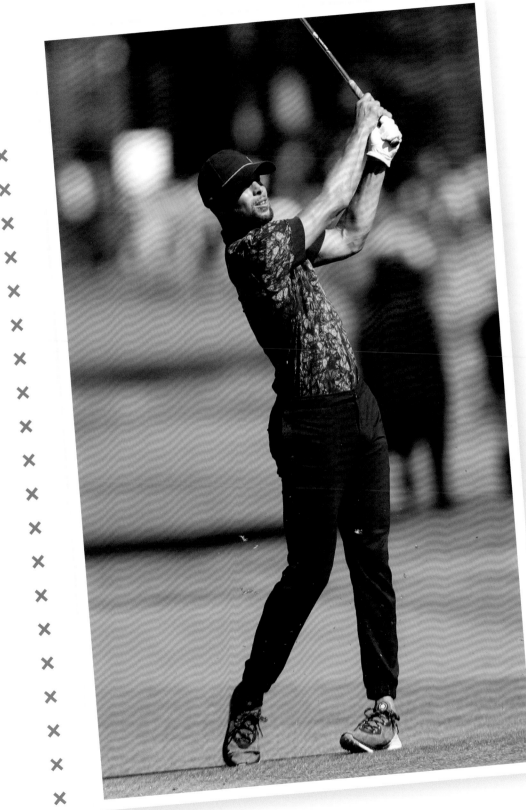

CURRY'S
MVPS

Steph and Ayesha met in a church youth group. They were just teenagers. Talk about a meet-cute! Years later, they met again in Hollywood. They were a couple from then on.

Ayesha moved to Charlotte, North Carolina, to be close to Steph. He was playing basketball at Davidson College. They got married on July 30, 2011. The Currys have two daughters and a son.

For a long time, Steph Curry was the proud "girl dad" of his two daughters, Riley and Ryan.

Riley was born in 2012. She stole fans' hearts when she stole the show at Steph's **press conference** in 2015! That was also the year their second daughter, Ryan, was born.

FACT

Riley Curry is a volleyball player, just like her aunt and grandmother.

Fans wondered if the Currys would have a boy to pass down the Wardell name. Sure enough, on July 2, 2018, their baby boy was born. They named him Canon Wardell Jack Curry.

FACT
The name Canon means "young wolf."

GIVING
BACK

In 2022, Curry donated more than $100,000 to the Positive Coaching **Alliance**. This program trains middle-school basketball coaches.

Steph made a game of it. He agreed to give away $1,000 for every point he scored in the All-Star Game. He would add $10,000 if he was named the game's MVP. In the end, he gave away $108,000.

In 2016, Curry flew to Tanzania in East Africa. There, he gave tens of thousands of mosquito nets to families at a **refugee** camp. These nets hang from the ceiling over a bed. They keep mosquitoes away. Their bites can cause serious sickness. Steph hung up some of the nets himself.

A mosquito net.

A refugee camp
in Tanzania

Steph and Ayesha also started a **foundation** called Eat. Learn. Play. Its purpose is to create activities to help kids grow up healthy and strong. It focuses on eating healthy food. It also helps kids who struggle in school. The foundation makes sure kids have safe places to play in the city.

Glossary

alliance (uh-LY-uhnts)—an agreement between groups of people to work together

assassin (uh-SA-suhn)—a person who kills an important person, such as a president; in sports, refers to an aggressive top athlete

charity (CHAYR-uh-tee)—a group that raises money or collects goods to help people in need

foundation (foun-DAY-shuhn)—an organization that gives money to good causes

press conference (PRESS KAHN-frenss)—an event in which information is presented to reporters and questions are answered

refugee (ref-yuh-JEE)—a person who has been forced to leave his or her home to escape war or persecution

Read More

Curry, Stephen. *I Have a Superpower*. New York: Penguin Workshop, 2022.

Frederickson, Kevin. *Steph Curry*. Minnetonka, MN: Kaleidoscope Pub., Inc., 2019.

Hewson, Anthony K. *Golden State Warriors*. Minneapolis: Abdo Publishing, a division of ABDO, 2022.

Internet Sites

Biography: Stephen Curry
biography.com/athlete/stephen-curry

Meet NBA Star Steph Curry's Favorite Teammate—His Wife, Ayesha Curry!
parade.com/1369699/kaigreen/steph-curry-wife-ayesha-curry/

Stephen Curry's 47-point takeover delivers Warriors needed win
espn.com/nba/story/_/id/34977673/stephen-curry-47-point-take-over-delivers-warriors-needed-win

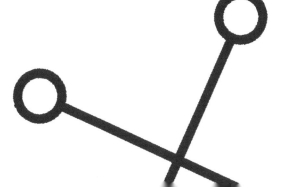

Index

All-Star Game, 24

college, 19

Eat. Learn. Play., 28

family, 5, 7, 8, 19
  Curry, Ayesha, 10, 12, 13, 19, 28
  Curry, Canon, 19, 23
  Curry, Dell, 6, 7
  Curry-Lee, Sydel, 8, 9
  Curry, Riley, 19, 20
  Curry, Ryan, 19, 20
  Curry, Seth, 8, 9

Curry, Sonya, 6, 7

golf, 16

Lee, Damion, 8, 9

McIlroy, Rory, 16

nicknames, 5

Obama, President Barack, 16

Positive Coaching Alliance, 24

snacks, 14

Thompson, Klay, 10

About the Author

Dr. Nafeesah Allen is a world traveler, wife, and mom of two. Her family speaks English, Spanish, and Portuguese, and has surprise dance parties in the kitchen.